631ART.COM PRESENTS:
"KOALA KINGDOM"
I0837677
BY EDDIE ALFARO

KOALAS
HAVE
LARGE
NOSES
THAT
ARE
COLOURED
PINK
OR BLACK.

THE REASON THE KOALA
IS CALLED A KOALA BEAR
IS BECAUSE THE KOALA
LOOKS LIKE A TEDDY BEAR.

KOALAS DON'T HAVE MUCH ENERGY AND, WHEN NOT FEASTING ON LEAVES, THEY SPEND THEIR TIME DOZING IN THE BRANCHES.

KOALAS HAVE A VERY SUPPORTIVE BUTT, THEY HAVE STRONG CARTILAGE AT THE END OF THEIR CURVED SPINE.

KOALAS SURVIVE ON A DIET OF EUCALYPTUS
LEAVES AND CAN EAT UP TO A KILOGRAM A DAY.

KOALAS ARE ONLY 25 TO 35 INCHES LONG,
AND WEIGH JUST 30 POUNDS OR LESS.

THE WORD KOALA MEANS "AN ANIMAL WHICH DOES NOT DRINK".

THEY ARE NOT VERY SOCIAL
ANIMALS AND USUALLY STAY ALONE.

KOALAS CAN SLEEP UP
TO 18 HOURS A DAY.

THE KOALA DO NOT BELONG TO
THE BEAR FAMILY IN ANY WAY.

A BABY KOALA WHICH HAS BEEN JUST BORN IS USUALLY LESS THAN 1 INCH LONG.

KOALAS HAVE
FINGERPRINTS
JUST LIKE HUMANS.

THEY HAVE DIFFERENT FUR
TYPE IN DIFFERENT AREAS.

EVERY MALE KOALA HAS A SCENT GLAND ON THE CHEST WHICH THEY RUB ON THE TREES TO MARK THEIR TERRITORIES.

KOALAS HAVE THEIR VERY OWN
DIGESTIVE ORGAN, KNOWN AS A "CAECUM".

IF NECESSARY KOALAS CAN BREAK INTO
A GALLOP, MOVING AT SPEEDS OF UP
TO 18 MILES PER HOUR.

KOALAS HAVE THICK, WOOLLY FUR WHICH ACTS LIKE A 'RAINCOAT' TO REPEL MOISTURE WHEN IT RAINS.

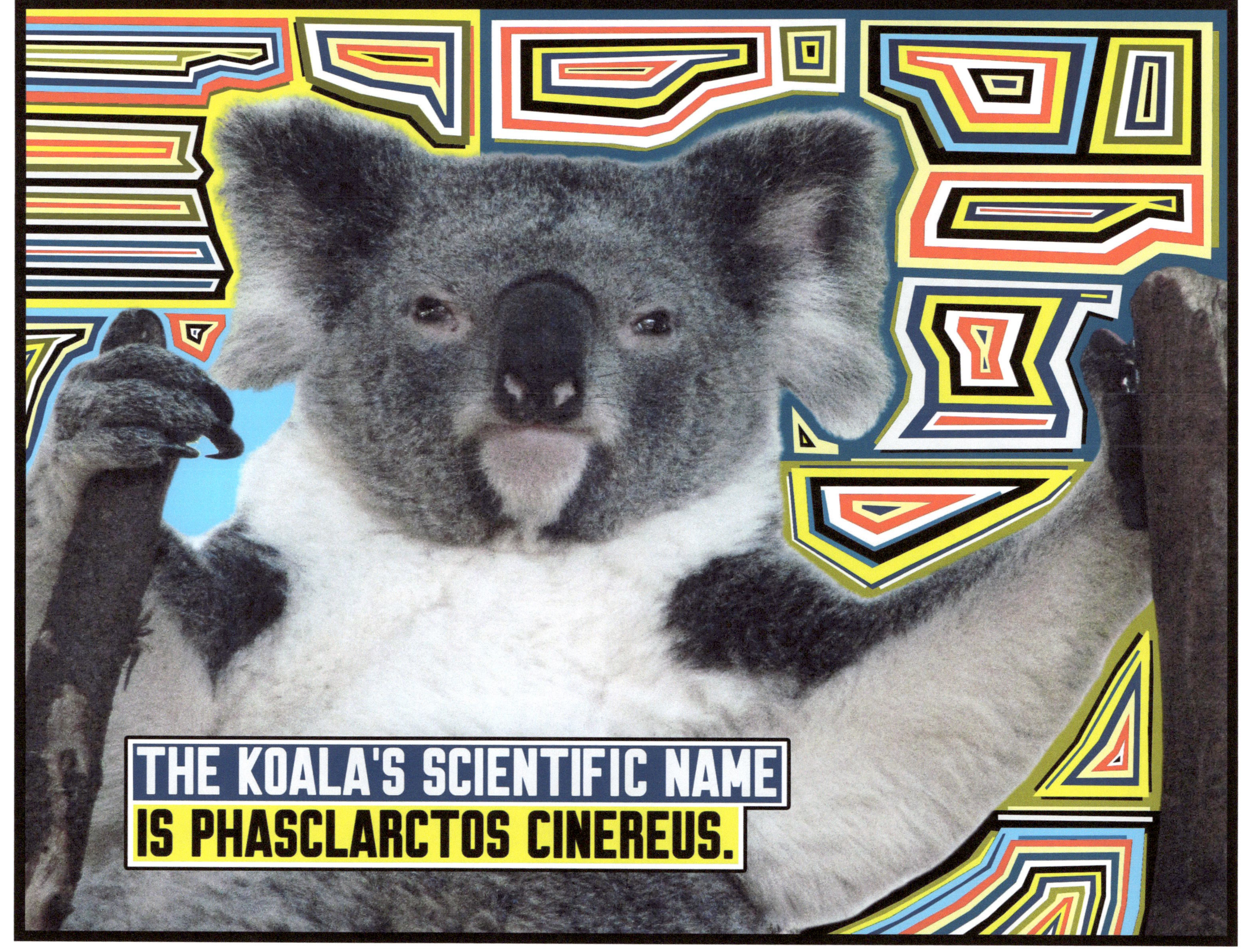
THE KOALA'S SCIENTIFIC NAME IS PHASCLARCTOS CINEREUS.

THANK YOU.
THE END.

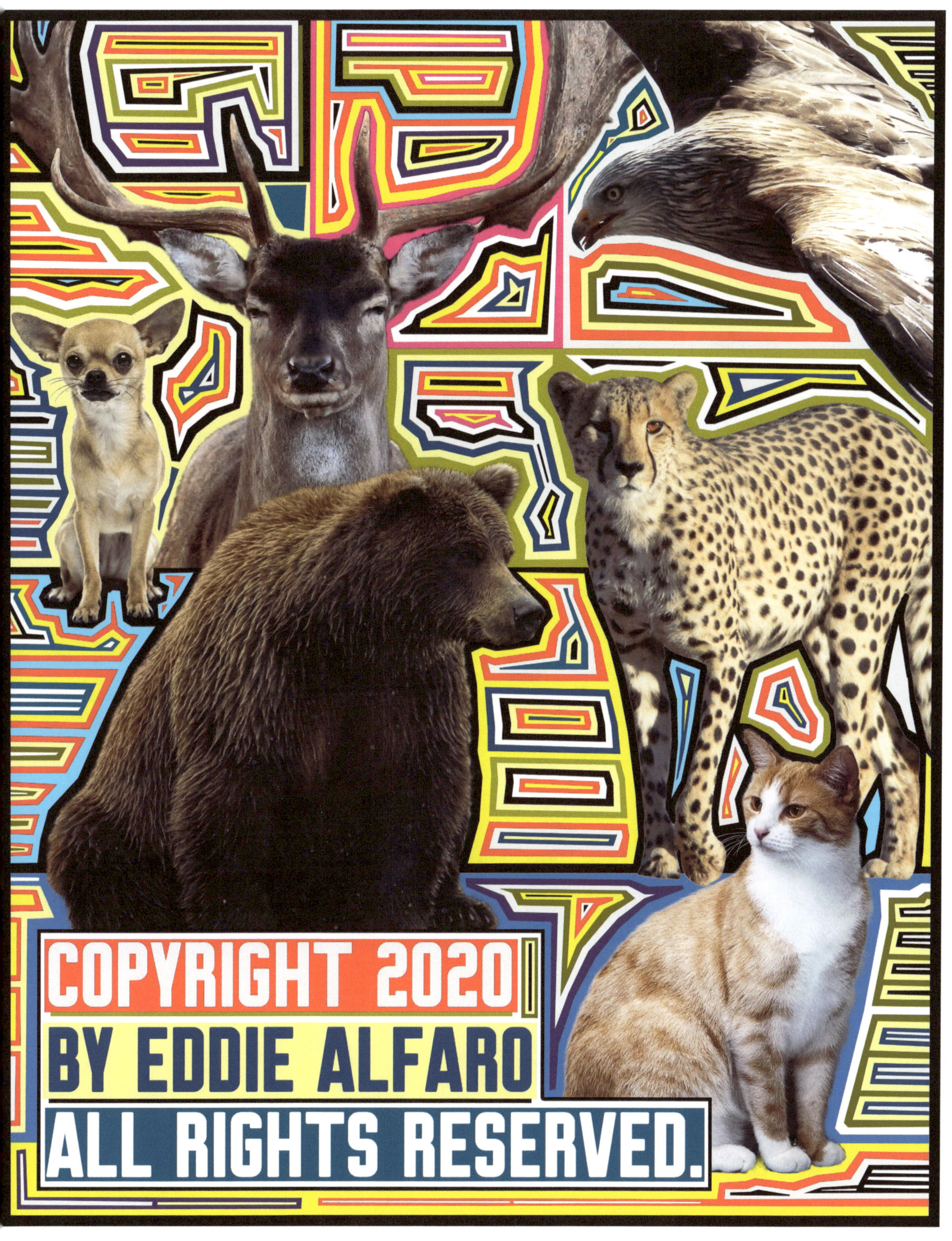
COPYRIGHT 2020
BY EDDIE ALFARO
ALL RIGHTS RESERVED.

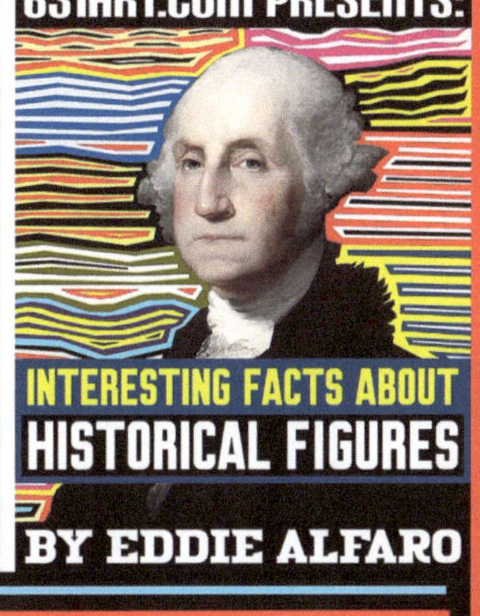

MORE BOOKS AT:

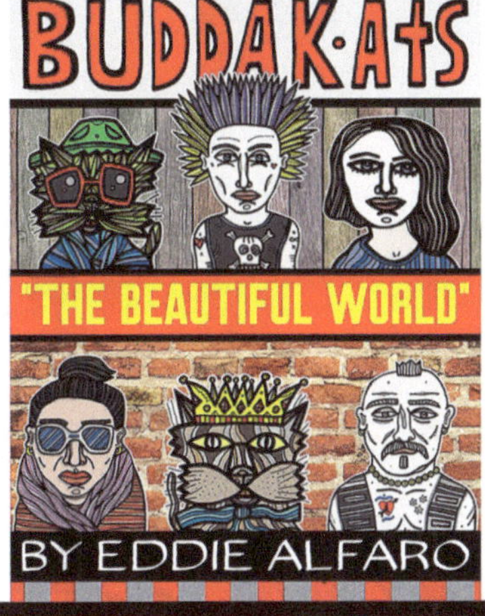